342.73 Wha
What rights should illegal
immigrants have? /

34028062211124
CYF $19.95 ocm64594512

HARRIS COUNTY PUBLIC LIBRARY

O9-BHJ-354

At Issue

What Rights Should Illegal Immigrants Have?

Other books in the At Issue series:

At Issue

What Rights Should Illegal Immigrants Have?

Lori Newman, Book Editor

GREENHAVEN PRESS

An imprint of Thomson Gale, a part of The Thomson Corporation

THOMSON
™
GALE

Bonnie Szumski, *Publisher*
Helen Cothran, *Managing Editor*

© 2006 Thomson Gale, a part of The Thomson Corporation.

Thomson and Star logo are trademarks and Gale and Greenhaven Press are registered trademarks used herein under license.

For more information, contact:
Greenhaven Press
27500 Drake Rd.
Farmington Hills, MI 48331-3535
Or you can visit our Internet site at http://www.gale.com

ALL RIGHTS RESERVED
No part of this work covered by the copyright hereon may be reproduced or used in any form or by any means—graphic, electronic, or mechanical, including photocopying, record-ing, taping, Web distribution, or information storage retrieval systems—without the written permission of the publisher.

Articles in Greenhaven Press anthologies are often edited for length to meet page require-ments. In addition, original titles of these works are changed to clearly present the main thesis and to explicitly indicate the author's opinion. Every effort is made to ensure that Greenhaven Press accurately reflects the original intent of the authors. Every effort has been made to trace the owners of copyrighted material.

Cover photograph reproduced by permission of Planet Art.

LIBRARY OF CONGRESS CATALOGING-IN-PUBLICATION DATA

What rights should illegal immigrants have? / Lori Newman, book editor.
    p. cm. -- (At issue)
  Includes bibliographical references and index.
  ISBN 0-7377-3480-9 (lib. : alk. paper) -- ISBN 0-7377-3481-7 (pbk. : alk. paper)
  1. Illegal aliens--Legal status, laws, etc.--United States. 2. Illegal aliens--Civil rights--United States. 3. Emigration and immigration law--United States.
4. Immigrants--United States. I. Newman, Lori M. II. At issue (San Diego, Calif.)
  KF4819.W53 2007
  342.7308'3--dc22
                              2006043415

Printed in the United States of America
10 9 8 7 6 5 4 3 2 1

Contents

Introduction

The United States owes much of its economic and technological success to the efforts of immigrants. According to the American Jewish Committee, "History has demonstrated that immigrants enrich this nation economically and culturally, and immigration remains a central ingredient to retaining America's economic strength." Nevertheless, the United States began limiting immigration in the early twentieth century. Some of these restrictions took the form of numerical quotas, while others sought to prevent immigration by restricting immigrants' right to work. The goal of the Immigration Reform and Control Act of 1986, for example, is to curb illegal immigration from Mexico by making it a crime for a U.S. employer to knowingly hire an undocumented worker—that is, one without papers to demonstrate citizenship or legal permission to work. The intent of this act was to make it difficult for undocumented workers to find jobs in the United States and thus discourage them from entering the country illegally to do so.

Despite such restrictions, the availability of jobs and relatively high wages continues to draw millions of undocumented workers to the United States. According to the activist Web site SpeakOut.com, Mexican immigrants can earn $60 per day in the United States for labor that would earn them only $5 a day in Mexico—the greatest wage gap between any two bordering countries in the world. The temptation of high earnings just across the border attracts many Mexicans to enter the United States illegally to work. Although Mexican workers consider $60 a high wage, American employees expect much higher wages. Paying the lower wage for illegal immigrant labor is therefore appealing to U.S. employers. Moreover, many immigrants are willing to work without receiving benefits such as health insurance, further lowering costs to U.S. employers who hire them. As a result, many U.S. employers are replacing American workers with lower-cost immigrant laborers. Some critics contend that illegal immigrants take jobs away from American workers, but other commentators argue that immigrants perform jobs that Americans are unwilling to perform. Whether U.S. employers should be punished for knowingly hiring illegal immigrants is subject to debate. This controversy reflects the greater debate over what rights illegal immigrants should have.

Those who believe that U.S. employers should be punished for hiring illegal immigrants argue that these immigrants take jobs away from American citizens. The cofounder of Connecticut Citizens for Immigration Control claims that his objections to illegal immigration "concern primarily . . . the loss of jobs for U.S. citizens." Columnist Joe Guzzardi agrees: "All across America, illegal immigrants are doing jobs once held by Americans." Those who oppose the employment of illegal immigrants also contend that the abundance of illegal immigrants in the U.S. workforce causes an overall reduction in wages, particularly for low-skilled jobs such as picking fruit. According to the Century Foundation's report *Immigration, Jobs, and the American Economy*, "immigration has somewhat reduced the wages of native-born workers, with less-skilled and less-educated individuals experiencing the most significant declines." The loss of jobs to illegal immigrants and the resulting overall reduction in wages, these commentators claim, is a strong argument for tighter restrictions on illegal immigrants and the employers who hire them.

Analysts who support the employment of illegal immigrants argue that they fill jobs that Americans refuse to perform. According to the North American Conference on Latin America (NACLA), "unauthorized immigrants fill relatively undesirable jobs only after [native] workers migrate into more desirable occupations." In 2004 President George W. Bush proposed a guest worker program to grant temporary U.S.

work visas to noncitizens, claiming, "If an American employer is offering a job that American citizens are not willing to take, we ought to welcome into our country a person who will fill that job." Proponents of this view believe that immigrants who perform undesirable, yet essential jobs improve the American economy. These analysts also assert that illegal immigrant workers do not lower U.S. wages in any significant way. In the report *Immigration and Immigrants: Setting the Record Straight*, Michael E. Fix and Jeffrey S. Passel of the Urban Institute cite studies that find "no strong evidence that immigration reduces overall availability of jobs or wages." The 2005 *Economic Report of the President*, a yearly report compiled by the president's economic advisers, contains several supporting examples. During the Mariel boatlift, for example, 125,000 Cubans, including 45,000 laborers, entered Miami over four months in 1980, with no resulting changes in wages or unemployment rates.

Whether illegal immigrant workers have a positive or negative impact on the U.S. economy remains controversial, as are the views on illegal immigrant rights expressed by the authors in the following volume. For many commentators, the employment of illegal immigrants remains a focal point of the debate over illegal immigrant rights, as the U.S. government works to improve border security and tighten immigration laws in the wake of the September 11, 2001, terrorist attacks. According to the 2005 *Economic Report of the President*, "The persistence of undocumented immigration and problems with employment-based immigration suggest that current policy falls short in addressing the demand for immigrant workers and the need for national security." Whether future policies will meet these competing needs remains to be seen.

1

Illegal Immigrants Have the Right to Receive U.S. Health Care

James Dwyer

James Dwyer is assistant professor of bioethics and humanities at the State University of New York Upstate Medical University. His research focuses on the connection between social conditions and public health.

The United States has an ethical obligation to provide health care to illegal immigrants. Undocumented immigrant workers deserve health care as a reward for performing disagreeable and low-paying jobs that Americans are unwilling to do. Denying illegal immigrants access to health care could also threaten public health by leaving serious, contagious illnesses untreated. Simply being in the United States illegally is not a sufficient reason to be denied needed health care.

Illegal immigrants form a large and disputed group in many countries. Indeed, even the name is in dispute. People in this group are referred to as illegal immigrants, illegal aliens, irregular migrants, undocumented workers, or, in French, as *sans papiers*. Whatever they are called, their existence raises an important ethical question: Do societies have an ethical responsibility to provide health care for them and to promote their health?

James Dwyer, "Illegal Immigrants, Health Care, and Social Responsibility," *The Hastings Center Report*, vol. 34, January-February 2004, p. 34. Copyright 2004 Hastings Center. Reproduced by permission.

Medical Care for Illegals Is an Ethical Question

This question often elicits two different answers. Some people—call them nationalists—say that the answer is obviously no. They argue that people who have no right to be in a country should not have rights to benefits in that country. Other people—call them humanists—say that the answer is obviously yes. They argue that all people should have access to health care. It's a basic human right.

I think both these answers are off the mark. The first focuses too narrowly on what we owe people based on legal rules and formal citizenship. The other answer focuses too broadly, on what we owe people qua human beings. We need a perspective that is in between, that adequately responds to the phenomenon of illegal immigration and adequately reflects the complexity of moral thought. There may be important ethical distinctions, for example, among the following groups: U.S. citizens who lack health insurance, undocumented workers who lack health insurance in spite of working full time, medical visitors who fly to the United States as tourists in order to obtain care at public hospitals, foreign citizens who work abroad for subcontractors of American firms, and foreign citizens who live in impoverished countries. I believe that we—U.S. citizens—have ethical duties in all of these situations, but I see important differences in what these duties demand and how they are to be explained.

In this paper, I want to focus on the situation of illegal immigrants. I will discuss several different answers to the question about what ethical responsibility we have to provide health care to illegal immigrants. . . .

I believe that a sound ethical response to the question of illegal immigration requires some understanding of the work that illegal immigrants do. Most undocumented workers do the jobs that citizens often eschew. They do difficult and disagreeable work at low wages for small firms in the informal

11

sector of the economy. In general, they have the worst jobs and work in the worst conditions in such sectors of the economy as agriculture, construction, manufacturing, and the food industry. They pick fruit, wash dishes, move dirt, sew clothes, clean toilets. . . .

A Matter of Desert

The abstract ethical question of whether societies have a responsibility to provide health care for illegal immigrants sometimes becomes a concrete political issue. Rising health care costs, budget reduction programs, and feelings of resentment sometimes transform the ethical question into a political debate. This has happened several times in the United States. In 1996, the Congress debated and passed the "Illegal Immigration Reform and Immigrant Responsibility Act." This law made all immigrants ineligible for Medicaid, although it did allow the federal government to reimburse states for emergency treatment of illegal immigrants. . . .

Although it is true that illegal aliens have violated a law by entering or remaining in the country, it is not clear what the moral implication of this point is. Nothing about access to health care follows from the mere fact that illegal aliens have violated a law. Many people break many different laws. Whether a violation of a law should disqualify people from public services probably depends on the nature and purpose of the services, the nature and the gravity of the violation, and many other matters.

Consider one example of a violation of the law. People sometimes break tax laws by working off the books. They do certain jobs for cash in order to avoid paying taxes or losing benefits. Moreover, this practice is probably well quite common. I recently asked students in two of my classes if they or anyone in their extended family had earned money that was not reported as taxable income. In one class, all but two students raised their hands. In the other class, every hand went up.

What is false is the idea that we have to choose between basic health care for illegal aliens and basic health care for citizens.

No one has suggested that health care facilities deny care to people suspected of working off the books. But undocumented work is also a violation of the law. Furthermore, it involves an issue of fairness because it shifts burdens onto others and diminishes funding for important purposes. Of course, working off the books and working without a visa are not alike in all respects. But without further argument, nothing much follows about whether it is right to deny benefits to people who have violated a law. . . .

I would restate the argument in the following way: Given the limited public budget for health care, U.S. citizens and legal residents are more deserving of benefits than are illegal aliens. This argument frames the issue as a choice between competing goods in a situation of limited resources.

There is something right and something wrong about this way of framing the issue. What is right is the idea that in all of life, individual and political, we have to choose between competing goods. A society cannot have everything: comprehensive and universal health care, good public schools, extensive public parks and beaches, public services, and very low taxes. What is false is the idea that we have to choose between basic health care for illegal aliens and basic health care for citizens. Many other tradeoffs are possible, including an increase in public funding.

The narrow framework of the debate pits poor citizens against illegal aliens in a battle for health care resources. Within this framework, the issue is posed as one of desert [who is most deserving of receiving a benefit]. Avoiding the idea of desert is impossible. After all, justice is a matter of giving people their due—giving them what they deserve. But a narrow conception of desert seems most at home in allocating particular goods that go beyond basic needs, in situations where the criteria of achievement and effort are very clear. For example, if we are asked to give an award for the best student in chemistry, a narrow notion of desert is appropriate and useful. But publicly funded health care is different and requires a broader view of desert.

Measures that deny care to illegal aliens, or make them afraid to seek care, could lead to an increase in tuberculosis.

The discussion of restrictive measures often focuses on desert, taxation, and benefits. Proponents tend to picture illegal immigrants as free riders who are taking advantage of public services without contributing to public funding. Opponents are quick to note that illegal immigrants do pay taxes. They pay sales tax, gas tax, and value-added tax. They often pay income tax and property tax. But do they pay enough tax to cover the cost of the services they use? Or more generally, are illegal immigrants a net economic gain or a net economic loss for society?

Instead of trying to answer the economic question, I want to point out a problem with the question itself. The question about taxation and benefits tends to portray society as a private business venture. On the business model, investors should benefit in proportion to the funds they put into the venture. This may be an appropriate model for some business ventures, but it is not an adequate model for all social institutions and benefits. The business model is not an adequate model for thinking about voting, legal defense, library services, minimum wages, occupational safety, and many other social benefits. . . .

A Matter of Professional Ethics

Some of the most vigorous responses to restrictive measures have come from those who consider the issue within the framework of professional ethics. Tal Ann Ziv and Bernard Lo, for example, argue [in the *New England Journal of Medicine*] that "cooperating with Proposition 187 [a proposal to deny health care to illegal immigrants in California] would undermine professional ethics." In particular, they argue that cooperating with this kind of restrictive measure is inconsistent with physicians' "ethical responsibilities to protect the public health, care for persons in medical need, and respect patient confidentiality."

Restrictive measures may indeed have adverse effects on the public health. For example, measures that deny care to illegal aliens, or make them afraid to seek care, could lead to an increase in tuberculosis. And physicians do have a professional obligation to oppose measures that would significantly harm the public health. . . .

A Matter of Social Responsibility

Framing the issue in terms of social responsibility helps to highlight one of the most striking features of illegal immigration: the employment pattern within society. As I noted before, illegal immigrants often perform the worst work for the lowest wages. Illegal immigrants are part of a pattern that is older and deeper than the recent globalization of the economy. Societies have often used the most powerless and marginalized people to do the most disagreeable and difficult work. Societies have used slaves, indentured servants, castes, minorities, orphans, poor children, internal migrants, and foreign migrants. Of course, the pattern is not exactly the same in every society, nor even in every industry within a society, but the similarities are striking.

I see the use of illegal immigrants as the contemporary form of the old pattern. But it is not a natural phenomenon beyond human control. It is the result of laws, norms, institutions, habits, and conditions in society, and of the conditions in the world at large. It is a social construction that we could try to reconstruct.

Some might object that no one forces illegal immigrants to take unsavory jobs and that they can return home if they wish. This objection is too simple. Although most undocumented workers made a voluntary choice to go to another country, they often had inadequate information and dismal alternatives, and voluntary return is not an attractive option when they have substantial debts and poor earning potential at home. More importantly, even a fully informed and voluntary choice does not settle the question of social justice and responsibility. . . .

We need to take responsibility for preventing the old pattern from continuing, and the key idea is that of "taking responsibility. . . ."

An Inclusive View of Society

Why should society take responsibility for people it tried to keep out of its territory, for people who are not social members? Because in many respects illegal immigrants are social members. Although they are not citizens or legal residents, they may be diligent workers, good neighbors, concerned parents, and active participants in community life. They are workers, involved in complex schemes of social cooperation. Many of the most exploited workers in the industrial revolution—children, women, men without property—were also not full citizens, but they were vulnerable people, doing often undesirable work, for whom society needed to take some responsibility. Undocumented workers' similar role in society is one reason that the social responsibility to care for them is different from the responsibility to care for medical visitors.

> *Providing health care for all workers ... [will] improve the benefit that workers receive ... and ... express social and communal respect for them.*

If a given society had the ethical conviction and political will, it could develop practical measures to transform the worst aspects of some work, empower the most disadvantaged workers, and shape the background conditions in which the labor market operates. The interests of the worst-off citizens and the interests of illegal immigrants need not be opposed. Practical measures may raise labor costs and increase the price of goods and services, as they should. We should not rely on undocumented workers to keep down prices on everything from strawberries to sex. . . .

Good health care can, among other things, prevent death and suffering, promote health and well-being, respond to basic needs and vulnerabilities, express care and solidarity, contribute to equality of opportunity, monitor social problems (such as child abuse or pesticide exposure), and accomplish other important aims. But health care is just one means, and not always the most effective means, to these ends. To focus on access to and payment of health care is to focus our ethical concern too narrowly.

I believe that societies that attract illegal immigrants should pursue policies and practices that (1) improve the pay for and conditions of the worst forms of work; (2) structure and organize work so as to give workers more voice, power, and opportunity to develop their capacities; and (3) connect labor to unions, associations, and communities in ways that increase social respect for all workers. I cannot justify these claims in this paper, but I want to note how they are connected to health care. Providing health care for all workers

17

and their families is a very good way to improve the benefit that workers receive for the worst forms of work, to render workers less vulnerable, and to express social and communal respect for them. These are good reasons for providing health care for all workers, documented and undocumented alike. And they express ethical concerns that are not captured by talking about human rights, public health, or the rights of citizens.

I have examined the frameworks that are employed in discussions about illegal immigrants and health care. I argued against conceptualizing the issues in terms of [deserting,] . . . professional ethics, or even human rights. Although all of these concepts highlight something important, they tend to be too narrow or too broad. . . .

[My goal is] to shift the discussion into the realm of social justice and responsibility.

2

Illegal Immigrants Threaten U.S. Health Care

Madeline Pelner Cosman

Madeline Pelner Cosman, a medical lawyer, is president of Medical Equity, Inc., a national medical and law practice brokerage located in San Diego, California.

A flood of illegal immigrants threatens the U.S. health care system and public health. Several California hospitals have gone bankrupt providing free health care to illegal aliens. Anchor babies—illegal immigrant babies born in the United States that are automatically granted U.S. citizenship—have increased Medicaid and other benefit program costs. Illegal immigrants also bring dangerous diseases such as tuberculosis and leprosy that have not been seen in the United States for many years. To save America's health care system, the United States must tighten its borders, revoke the automatic citizenship of anchor babies, punish those who help illegal aliens, and stop granting amnesty.

The influx of illegal aliens has serious hidden medical consequences. We judge reality primarily by what we see. But what we do not see can be more dangerous, more expensive, and more deadly than what is seen.

Illegal aliens' stealthy assaults on medicine now must rouse Americans to alert and alarm. Even President Bush describes illegal aliens only as they are seen: strong physical laborers who work hard in undesirable jobs with low wages, who care for their families, and who pursue the American dream.

Madeline Pelner Cosman, "Illegal Aliens and American Medicine," *Journal of American Physicians and Surgeons*, vol. 10, spring 2005, pp. 6-10. Reproduced by permission.

The Hidden Cost of Illegal Workers

What is unseen is their free medical care that has degraded and closed some of America's finest emergency medical facilities, and caused hospital bankruptcies: 84 California hospitals are closing their doors. "Anchor babies" born to illegal aliens instantly qualify as citizens for welfare benefits and have caused enormous rises in Medicaid costs and stipends under Supplemental Security Income [SSI] and Disability Income.

What is seen is the illegal alien who with strong back may cough, sweat, and bleed, but is assumed healthy even though he and his illegal alien wife and children were never examined for contagious diseases.

By default, we grant health passes to illegal aliens. Yet many illegal aliens harbor fatal diseases that American medicine fought and vanquished long ago, such as drug-resistant tuberculosis, malaria, leprosy, plague, polio, dengue, and Chagas disease.

What is seen is the political statistic that 43 million lives are at risk in America because of lack of medical insurance. What is unseen is that medical insurance does not equal medical care. Uninsured people receive medical care in hospital emergency departments (EDs) under the coercive Emergency Medical Treatment and Active Labor Act of 1985 (EMTALA), which obligates hospitals to treat the uninsured but does not pay for that care. Also unseen is the percentage of the uninsured who are illegal aliens. No one knows how many illegal aliens reside in America. If there are 10 million, they constitute nearly 25 percent of the uninsured. The percentage could be even higher.

EMTALA's Impact

The Emergency Medical Treatment and Active Labor Act (EMTALA) requires every ED to treat anyone who enters with an "emergency," including cough, headache, hangnail, cardiac arrest, herniated lumbar disc, drug addiction, alcohol overdose, gunshot wound, automobile trauma, human immunodeficiency virus (HIV)-positive infection, mental problem, or personality disorder.

Illegal alien women come to the hospital in labor and drop their little anchors, each of whom pulls its [entire family] into permanent residency.

The definition of emergency is flexible and vague enough to include almost any condition. Any patient coming to a hospital ED requesting "emergency" care must be screened and treated until ready for discharge, or stabilized for transfer—whether or not insured, "documented," or able to pay. A woman in labor must remain to deliver her child.

The hospital must have specialists on call at all times for all departments that provide medical services and specialties within the hospital's capabilities. EMTALA is an unfunded federal mandate. Government imposes viciously stiff fines and penalties on any physician and any hospital refusing to treat any patient that a zealous prosecutor deems an emergency patient, even though the hospital or physician screened and declared the patient's illness or injury non-emergency. But government pays neither hospital nor physician for treatments. . . .

As many as 10,000 illegals cross the 1,940-mile-long border with Mexico each day. About 33 percent are caught. Many try again, immediately. Authorities estimate about 3,500 illegal aliens daily become permanent U.S. residents—at least 3 million annually. EMTALA rewards them with extensive, expensive medical services, free of charge, if they claim an emergency need for care. Government welcomes illegal aliens by refusal to police our borders, by reluctance to prosecute people who violate basic American law, and by fervor to please those who abuse our generosity and cynically ply our compassion against us.

Anchor Babies

American hospitals welcome "anchor babies." Illegal alien women come to the hospital in labor and drop their little anchors, each of whom pulls its illegal alien mother, father, and siblings into permanent residency simply by being born within our borders. Anchor babies are *citizens*, and instantly qualify for public welfare aid. Between 300,000 and 350,000 anchor babies annually become citizens because of the Fourteenth Amendment to the U.S. Constitution: "All persons born or naturalized in the United States, and subject to the jurisdiction thereof, are citizens of the United States and the State wherein they reside."

In 2003 in Stockton, California, 70 percent of the 2,300 babies born in San Joaquin General Hospital's maternity ward were anchor babies, and 45 percent of Stockton children under age six are Latino (up from 30 percent in 1993). In 1994, 74,987 anchor babies in California hospital maternity units cost $215 million and constituted 36 percent of all Medi-Cal [California's public health care funding] births. Now they account for substantially more than half. . . .

Illegal aliens have translators, advocates, and middlemen supplied by immigrants' civil rights groups or by Medicaid. MediCal in 2003 had 760,000 illegal aliens, up from 2002 when there were 470,000. Supplemental Security Income is a non-means-tested federal grant of money and food stamps. People qualify easily. Scams, frauds, and cheats are rampant. In one clinic, 300 people diagnosed as "mildly mentally retarded" all had the same translator, same psychiatrist, same symptoms, and similar stipend. Fraud is an equal-opportunity employer that flouts America's generosity to the feeble, the crippled, and the poor. Illegal aliens have powerful legal facilitators who litigate and lobby for "Open Borders" and for welfare benefits for all who cross onto America's soil. Open Borders proponents imperil America's sovereignty by obliterating distinctions between legal immigrants and illegal aliens, and between American citizens and all other people of the hungry world. . . .

Social Security Income [SSI] Payments Are Out of Control

Drug addiction and alcoholism [DA&A] are classified as diseases and disabilities. Disability Code DA&A had in 1983 only 3,000 stipend recipients, but in 1994 exploded to 101,000. In 2003, between 250,000 and 400,000 got lump-sum grants of disability money via SSI. When [immigrant] Linda Torres was arrested in Bakersfield, California, with about $8,500 in small bills in a sack, the police originally thought it was stolen money. It was her SSI lump sum award for her disability: heroin addiction.

Illegal aliens simply cross our borders medically unexamined, hiding . . . communicable diseases.

Immigrants on SSI, including legal aliens, refugees, and illegals with fraudulent Social Security cards, numbered a mere 127,900 aliens (3.3 percent of recipients) in 1982. By 1992 the numbers expanded to 601,430 entitled (10.9 percent of recipients). In 2003, this figure was several million (about 25 percent of recipients).

The National Immigration Law Center (NILC) proudly announced that it garnered for immigrants expensive cancer treatments, prenatal care, and critical health services by means of its litigation. Sometimes NILC worked in collaboration with lawyers from the American Civil Liberties Union and the Mexican American Legal Defense and Education Fund. Though the 1996 Welfare Reform Legislation reduced all welfare payments to all recipients nationwide, NILC cleverly managed to restore to its constituency of legal and illegal immigrants: $12 billion in Supplemental Security Income, and more than $800 million in food stamps. For many illegal aliens, America is land of the victim and home of the entitled.

Illegal Immigrants Bring Contagious Diseases

When my grandfather came to America, he first kissed the ground of New York's Ellis Island, then he stripped naked and coughed hard. Every legal immigrant before 1924 was examined for infectious diseases upon arrival and tested for tuberculosis. Anyone infected was shipped back to the old country. That was powerful incentive for each newcomer to make heroic efforts to appear healthy. Today *legal* immigrants must demonstrate that they are free of communicable diseases and drug addiction to qualify for lawful permanent residency green cards. Illegal aliens simply cross our borders medically unexamined, hiding in their bodies any number of communicable diseases.

Leprosy is now endemic to northeastern states because illegal aliens and other immigrants brought leprosy.

Many illegals who cross our borders have tuberculosis [TB]. That disease had largely disappeared from America, thanks to excellent hygiene and powerful modern drugs such as isoniazid and rifampin. TB's swift, deadly return now is lethal for about 60 percent of those infected because of new Multi-Drug Resistant Tuberculosis (MDR-TB). Until recently MDR-TB was endemic to Mexico. This *Mycobacterium tuberculosis* is resistant to at least two major antitubercular drugs. Ordinary TB usually is cured in six months with four drugs that cost about $2,000. MDR-TB takes 24 months with many expensive drugs that cost around $250,000, with toxic side effects. Each illegal with MDR-TB coughs and infects 10 to 30 people, who will not show symptoms immediately. Latent disease explodes later.

TB was virtually absent in Virginia until in 2002, when it spiked a 17 percent increase, but Prince William County, just south of Washington, D.C., had a much larger rise of 188 percent. Public health officials blamed immigrants. In 2001 the Indiana School of Medicine studied an outbreak of MDR-TB, and traced it to Mexican illegal aliens. The Queens, New York, health department attributed 81 percent of new TB cases in 2001 to immigrants. The Centers for Disease Control and Prevention ascribed 42 percent of all new TB cases to "foreign born" people who have up to eight times higher incidence. Apparently, 66 percent of all TB cases coming to America originate in Mexico, the Philippines, and Vietnam. Virulent TB outbreaks afflicted schoolteachers and children in Michigan, adults and children in Texas, and policemen in Minnesota. Recently TB erupted in Portland, Maine, and Del Rey Beach, Florida.

Once-Rare Diseases Resurge

Chagas disease, also called American trypanosomiasis or "kissing bug disease," is transmitted by the reduviid bug, which prefers to bite the lips and face. The protozoan parasite that it carries, *Trypanosoma cruzi*, infects 18 million people annually in Latin America and causes 50,000 deaths. This disease also infiltrates America's blood supply. Chagas affects blood transfusions and transplanted organs. No cure exists. Hundreds of blood recipients may be silently infected. After 10 to 20 years, up to 30 percent will die when their hearts or intestines, enlarged and weakened by Chagas, burst. Three people in 2001 received Chagas-infected organ transplants. Two died.

Leprosy, a scourge in Biblical days and in medieval Europe, so horribly destroys flesh and faces it was called the "disease of the soul." Lepers quarantined in leprosaria sounded noisemakers when they ventured out to warn people to stay far away. Leprosy, Hansen's disease, was so rare in America that in 40 years only 900 people were afflicted. Suddenly, [since 2002] America has more than 7,000 cases of leprosy. Leprosy now is endemic to northeastern states because illegal aliens and other immigrants brought leprosy from India, Brazil, the Caribbean, and Mexico.

Dengue fever is exceptionally rare in America, though common in Ecuador, Peru, Vietnam, Thailand, Bangladesh, Malaysia, and Mexico. Recently there was a virulent outbreak of dengue fever in Webb County, Texas, which borders Mexico. Though dengue is usually not a fatal disease, dengue hemorrhagic fever routinely kills.

America's inadequate federal border enforcement permits massive daily border penetrations that violate the integrity of our medicine.

Polio was eradicated from America, but now reappears in illegal immigrants, as do intestinal parasites. Malaria was obliterated, but now is re-emerging in Texas. About 4,000 children under age five annually in America develop fever, red eyes, "strawberry tongue," and acute inflammation of their coronary arteries and other blood vessels because of the infectious malady called Kawasaki disease. Many suffer heart attacks and sudden death.

Hepatitis A, B, and C, are resurging. Asians number 4 percent of Americans, but account for more than half of Hepatitis B cases. Why inoculate *all* American newborns for Hepatitis B when most infected persons are Asians?

A Proposal to Protect U.S. Citizens

Tough medicine could end the cataclysm in American medicine. I suggest the acronym CRAG for four critical actions to reclaim America's EDs; to restore medicine's proud scientific excellence and profitability; and to protect Americans against bacterial, viral, parasitic, and fungal infectious diseases that illegal aliens carry across our borders.

Close America's borders. Prevent illegal entry with fences, high-tech security devices, and troops re-deployed from Germany and South Korea. Deport illegal aliens. . . .

Internment and deportation are politically incorrect. But America's inadequate federal border enforcement permits massive daily border penetrations that violate the integrity of our medicine and our national security.

Rescind the citizenship of anchor babies. We must overturn the misinterpretation of the Fourteenth Amendment to the U.S. Constitution. The Constitution grants citizenship to all persons born or naturalized in the United States and *"subject to the jurisdiction thereof."* An illegal alien mother is subject to the jurisdiction of her *home* country. The baby of an illegal alien mother also is subject to that home country's jurisdiction.

When the Fourteenth Amendment was ratified, its purpose was to assure rights of freedom and citizenship to newly emancipated Negro citizens. American Indians, however, were excluded from American citizenship because of their tribal jurisdiction. Also not subject to American jurisdiction were foreign visitors, ambassadors, consuls, and their babies born here. For citizenship, the person was required to submit to complete, exclusive American jurisdiction, owing allegiance to no other nation. . . .

Congress by legislation has the right to create uniform rules on naturalization, and to create dual citizenship and similar variations upon "jurisdiction." We must be vigilant against congressmen voting to extend the list of those born here to include illegal aliens or other lawbreakers, conferring American citizenship and its generous social and medical benefits on babies born to criminals. It is irrelevant that some lawbreakers are hard-working women willing to do hard jobs for low pay, or that they are wives, daughters, cousins, lovers, or concubines of men willing to do America's hard work. Gravid wombs should not guarantee free medical care and instant infant citizenship in America. We must reestablish the original limits on citizenship, and remove incentives for indigent Mexicans and others to break America's immigration law. Proud legal immigrants applaud order, reason, and law.

Aiding and abetting illegal aliens is a crime. Punish it. This will anger devotees of illegal aliens who believe that the Constitution guarantees them civil rights that trump American administrative, civil, and criminal laws.

Grant no new amnesties. We must choose either to surrender medicine to illegal aliens, or to fight illegal aliens. Surrender to illegal aliens is surrender to collectivist America: land of moral ambiguity and home of pacifist appeasement. Fighting against illegal aliens is fighting for individualistic America: land of moral strength, and home of responsible liberty.

As we fight to reclaim medicine, so we defend our nation.

3

Illegal Immigrants in the U.S. Military Should Be Granted Citizenship

Max Boot

The Development, Relief, and Education for Alien Minors (DREAM) Act would offer legal status and citizenship eligibility to undocumented immigrant children upon their completion of two years of college or two years' service in the armed forces. Immigrants who serve in the U.S. military would develop a strong bond to the United States. In addition, such a program would by its nature select those who have the motivation and work ethic that Americans value.

Editor's note: The DREAM Act was reintroduced in the Senate in November 2005. As of this writing, it had not passed.

The US Army is getting desperate. Having fallen 25 percent short of already reduced [May 2005] recruiting goals . . . it is raising enlistment bonuses to US$40,000 in some cases and lowering standards to accept and retain soldiers who would have been turned away in years past. A minor criminal record? No high school diploma? Uncle Sam still wants you.

With combat dragging on in Iraq and plenty of jobs available at home, there aren't enough volunteers. So far, a real crisis has been averted only because the US Army has exceeded its retention goals and kept some troops in uniform past their discharge dates, but it will only get tougher to keep volunteers in uniform if troops are constantly deployed overseas.

Max Boot, "Fight for US Citizenship," *The Standard*, June 21, 2005. Copyright © *Los Angeles Times*. All rights reserved. Reproduced by permission of the author.

There are two obvious, and obviously wrongheaded, solutions to this problem: pull out of Iraq now or institute a draft. The former would hand a victory to terrorists and undo everything that more than 1,700 Americans have given their lives to achieve. The latter option, aside from being a political non-starter, would also dilute the high quality of an all-volunteer force.

[The United States should] offer citizenship to anyone, anywhere on the planet, willing to serve a set term in the U.S. military.

The Solution—Recruit Illegal Immigrants

I return to a solution I proposed in February [2005]: broadening the recruiting base beyond US citizens and permanent, legal residents. Legislation has been drafted to make a modest start in that direction.

The proposed Development, Relief and Education for Alien Minors [DREAM] Act is targeted at children of undocumented immigrants residing in the United States for more than five years but not born there.

They would get legal status and become eligible for citizenship if they graduate from high school, stay out of trouble and either attend college for two years or serve two years in the armed forces. This bill failed last year in the US Senate to get a floor vote. [The bill was reintroduced in November 2005.]

Broadening the Proposal

The DREAM Act is a great idea, but I would go further and offer citizenship to anyone, anywhere on the planet, willing to serve a set term in the US military. America could model a Freedom Legion after the French Foreign Legion. Or it could allow foreigners to join regular units after a period of English-language instruction, if necessary.

When I first made this suggestion, I got a lot of positive responses but also some scathing critiques. A retired army sergeant wrote (expletives deleted): "Are you out of your mind? The last thing we need in our military is a bunch of illegal immigrants serving in combat operations for a country to which they are not culturally bonded!" But there is no better way to build that bond than through military training and discipline. Drill sergeants have been forging cohesive units out of disparate elements since the days of the Roman legions.

Serving a few years in the military would . . . establish beyond a doubt that [foreigners] are the kind of motivated, hardworking immigrants the United States wants.

In the past, the US military had many more foreigners than it does today. (During the Civil War, at least 20 percent were immigrants. Now it's 7 percent.) The British army, among many others, has also made good use of noncitizens. Nepalese Gurkhas still fight and die for the Union Jack [British flag] despite not being "culturally bonded" to it. No doubt they would do the same for the Stars and Stripes.

Answering Critics' Fears

Some critics invoke the specter of mercenaries leading to the fall of the United States as they supposedly led to the fall of Rome. That's a misreading of Roman history. As classicist Victor Davis Hanson points out, by the 1st century AD, the legions "were mostly non-Italian and mercenary, and the empire still endured for nearly another 500 years." If only the Pax Americana were to last half as long! Other critics think it's repugnant to ask foreigners to face dangers that citizens won't. But there is always an element of unfairness in war. Unless you institute a truly universal draft, some will always be more at risk than others.

Besides, the US already makes ample use of mercenaries. It relies on tens of thousands of contractors in Iraq, Colombia and elsewhere, many of them not Americans. They would be a lot more useful if they were in uniform and subject to military orders.

The Best Alternative

Would foreigners sign up to fight for Uncle Sam? I don't see why not, because so many people are desperate to move [to the U.S.]. Serving a few years in the military would seem a small price to pay, and it would establish beyond a doubt that they are the kind of motivated, hardworking immigrants the United States wants.

Anyway, what's the alternative? US$100,000 signing bonuses? Recruiting felons?

4

Illegal Immigrants in the U.S. Military Should Not Be Granted Citizenship

Michael Ward

This editorial appeared in the Battalion, *a publication of Texas A&M University.*

The DREAM Act, which offers eligibility for permanent legal residence after finishing two years of college or military service, would provide illegal immigrants with undeserved benefits. Illegal aliens would be a military liability because their national loyalty is not clear. In addition, having entered the country illegally, they would be fighting to defend the very laws that they had broken. Such a proposal cheapens the idea of U.S. citizenship by making it easily attainable.

Editor's Note: The DREAM Act was reintroduced in the Senate in November 2005. As of this writing, it had not passed.

Everyone dreams, whether they can recall their dreams or not. Martin Luther King Jr. had a dream. REM's Michael Stipe claimed the eclectic lyrics of "It's the End of the World as We Know It" were inspired by a dream. Even [actor] Gary Coleman had a dream to one day live in a Sacramento mansion. But Orrin Hatch, the Republican senator from Utah, has a dream which would, while extending U.S. citizenship to illegal aliens, potentially grant them in-state tuition at public universities throughout the country.

Michael Ward, "DREAMing Big," *The Battalion*, Texas A & M University, November 5, 2003. Reproduced by permission.

This is not a dream; it sounds like a nightmare.

Co-sponsored by California Sen. Dianne Feinstein, Hatch's bill, according to *The Washington Times*, "would allow a six-year grace period for illegal immigrants who grew up in the United States and graduated from a U.S. high school, during which they would be exempt from deportation. If they finished two years of college or served two years in the military during that time, they could earn permanent legal residence in the United States." Also, according to *The Times*, the bill would allow states to grant illegal aliens in-state tuition at public colleges.

Abuse of U.S. Taxpayers' Money

If it sounds like the equivalent of homesteading for U.S. citizenship, it is. One wonders how long it took the politicians to convert "give illegal aliens benefits that most U.S. citizens don't receive" into the puffed-up, heart-wrenching "Development, Relief, and Education for Alien Minors," or DREAM, Act.[1]

With pressing issues facing U.S. citizens such as, say, a war on terror and a soft economy, the irresponsibility of this sort of legislation looms like a murky cloud over the shoulder of Hatch—and it stinks.

Military service is a product of citizenship, not a way to barter for it.

In a building paid for by U.S. taxpayers, politicians salaried by U.S. citizens are writing legislation that has the interests of illegal aliens at heart. Public officials have no right to draft legislation, the tangibility of which—to the average U.S. citizen—is so obscure as to be irrelevant. Legislation allocating funds for studying the viscosity of Heinz ketchup would be more responsible. At least it's an American company.

1. This bill failed in the Senate but was reintroduced in November 2005.

Citizenship Should Not Be a Reward for Military Service

But, moving past the irresponsible existence of the bill, one finds more foolishness: citizenship for military service. Given the arrest [in October 2003] of the Army's Ahmed Fathy Mehalba, a naturalized citizen and Arabic translator at Guantanamo Bay, Cuba, for illegally carrying classified documents through Boston's Logan Airport, it would seem the military is having enough trouble confirming the loyalties of its own citizen soldiers.

Yet, Hatch and Feinstein would like illegal aliens—those who have necessarily broken U.S. law—to serve equally alongside U.S. citizens as they then defend the laws they have broken. Military service is a product of citizenship, not a way to barter for it.

The DREAM Act would also repeal the federal prohibition on granting illegal aliens in-state tuition to public colleges. In other words, if one was from Mandeville, La., they would potentially have to pay almost twice as much as an illegal alien would to come to [Texas] A&M. "While I do not advocate granting unchecked amnesty to illegal immigrants," Hatch said, "I am in favor of providing children—children who did not make the decision to enter the United States illegally—the opportunity to earn the privilege of remaining here legally." By "earning" Hatch must mean "doing what you would normally do anyway."

Cheapening Citizenship

Keep in mind, the bill requires little more from illegal aliens than what they have been doing—residing in the United States. It is the United States that has the responsibility to grant citizenship. It's called homesteading and while it worked to build many states in this nation, it's a disservice to the idea of citizenship.

Instead of handing out citizenship, put the responsibility on immigrants. Perhaps, as Melissa Lazarin of the National Council of La Raza argues, "these young people were brought here by their parents, went to school here, speak English and consider this their country and essentially aren't able to demonstrate that."

Of course, the DREAM Act fails to mention any consequences imposed on the parents of the individuals who would take advantage of the legislation. Are they granted passive immunity from deportation? Probably—thus exponentially increasing the de facto effects of this legislation.

Nobody likes a bad dream. However, Hatch's dream is a bit too lucid for comfort. Perhaps a hard nudge and a perpetual caffeine drip would jar this dream from his mind and prevent similar ones from leaking onto the Senate floor. The DREAM Act is a nightmare. And, while the monster in the closet may not be real, this legislation is.

5

Undocumented Immigrants Are Entitled to In-State Tuition

Emmanuelle Le Texier

Emmanuelle Le Texier is a writer and researcher whose focus includes immigration, U.S.-Mexico relations, transnationalism, citizenship, and the mobilization of socially excluded people and immigrants.

Undocumented immigrants and their families in the United States deserve the same access to affordable education that U.S. citizens enjoy, including the right to pay in-state tuition. The children of undocumented immigrants have done nothing wrong by residing in the United States. In fact, these children work hard in school, speak the language, have assimilated, and should be rewarded with access to higher education. If the United States hopes to build a strong future, it must educate and train its diverse population.

[In 2003,] U.S. Representatives Howard Berman (D-California), Lucile Roybal-Allard (D-California) and Chris Cannon (R-Utah) proposed a bill in the House of Representatives called the Student Adjustment Act.[1] The U.S. Senate version is entitled the DREAM Act (Development, Relief and Education for Alien Minors). The DREAM Act would grant residency status to immigrants "of good moral character

1. This is the revised version of a similar bill proposed in 2001.

Emmanuelle Le Texier, "The Debate for In-state Tuition Fees Regardless of Immigration Status: The Right to Educate," *La Prensa San Diego*, May 9, 2003. Reproduced by permission.

between the ages of 12 and 21 who have lived in the United States for at least 5 years and to high school graduates under age 25 who are enrolled in a college or university." The Student Adjustment Act would do the same with students enrolled in seventh grade or above who have lived in the country for at least 5 years.

In brief, it would allow immigrants headed for colleges and universities, regardless of their immigration status, to be eligible to become U.S. residents and not have to pay out-of-state tuition fees. This legislation failed [in 2002] because [of] Republicans' opposition.

State-Level Initiatives

Nevertheless, in California, Utah, New York, and Texas, state legislatures have already approved similar plans before the federal law. But the debates are still very tense in other states. In Maryland, the legislation House Bill 1079 was sponsored by Gwendolyn Britt and Sheila Hixson (both Democrats) to allow undocumented students to attend public universities at in-state tuition rates. It passed both chambers on April 7, 2003, but Governor Ehrlich [vetoed it].

In Oregon, Peter Courtney (D) and Billy Dalto (R) sponsored Senate Bill 10 [to offer in-state tuition to] students who have attended high school in Oregon for more than three consecutive years, received a diploma and plan to become U.S citizens or legal residents.[2] On May 1 [2003], [Virginia] Governor [Mark R.] Warner vetoed HB 2339, legislation that intended to bar undocumented students from receiving in-state tuition rates in Virginia. On the opposite side [of the country], in Colorado, the House just overturned HB 1178, which call[ed] for in-state tuition. In Kansas, the Regents passed a

2. This bill passed in the Oregon Senate but failed in the House.

resolution on April 17, [2003], to endorse a House Bill that requires that the students have spent at least three years at a Kansas high school and have graduated or earned a GED to receive in-state tuition. The House passed the bill but the senate delayed the vote for 2004. [Fourteen] other states are debating similar legislation that has consequences on the most basic right: the right to education.

Opposing Arguments

The debates are intense because various organizations oppose [universal education], led in particular by think tanks like the Washington, D.C.–based Center for Immigration Studies (CIS) or the Federation for American Immigration Reform (FAIR). These groups also campaigned strongly against legislation that would allow undocumented immigrants the right to apply for driver's licenses and to exercise their right to work. They are also known for their vivid criticisms against the Mexican matricula consular, [the Mexican identity card given to Mexican nationals who live abroad] arguing that the Mexican consular ID card acceptance would mean an "amnesty for illegal aliens."

In Oregon, members of the anti-immigrant organization Oregonians for Immigration Reform said that a federal bill that would allow in-state tuition fees for students regardless of their immigration status is "rewarding law-breakers" and triggers a "demographic invasion," while others feared it would harm homeland security.

The fact that [undocumented immigrant] students cannot afford to pay out-[of-]state tuition should not be an impediment to education.

These arguments are not only unconvincing but also disrespectful of the basic right to education.

Countering the Criticism

First, the students who would qualify in this process would be rather marginal in numbers—an estimate of between 50,000 and 65,000 students could benefit from it countrywide.

Second, the students have not done anything illegal. They work hard at school; they are rewarded by the possibility of access to higher education. Their parents have lived in the U.S.; they pay taxes and are part of the community. These students for all intents and purpose are U.S. [citizens]: they were educated here, they speak the language, and they have adopted the culture, and are continuing the American dream seeking the highest education possible.

Third, the fact that students cannot afford to pay out-[of-]state tuition fees should not be an impediment to education.

The out-[of-]state tuition fees not only stop their dream of pursuing higher education but also violate the right to have access to education for children of immigrants' working-class families. In 1982, the U.S Supreme Court ruled "states must provide a free education through high school to children illegally in the country." This rule should be enforced at [the] college and university level by charging the lowest tuition fees possible for low-income immigrant families.

Fourth, prohibit[ing] access to higher education means that the country want[s] [n]either skilled workers [n]or educated citizens; [This] is nonsense when building the future of a country. During the celebration of the Dia del Niño, organized [in May 2003] by the Comité de Mujeres [(Women's Committee's)] Patricia Marin in Chicano Park, children sang: "Queremos paz y escuelas, no queremos guerra. We want peace and schools, no war."

Let's listen to the voice of these children; as they pointed out, [going] to school and university [represents] the basic right to education. They are entitled to it.

6

Colleges Should Not Offer Illegal Immigrants In-State Tuition

Joe Guzzardi

Joe Guzzardi, an English instructor in Lodi, California, frequently writes for the Lodi News-Sentinel *and CalNews.com.*

Illegal immigrants in the United States should not enjoy the right to pay lower in-state tuition rates. Permitting in-state tuition entices people to enter the country illegally, and in California such policies are compounding the state's already enormous debt. Moreover, it is unfair for an illegal immigrant to receive admission priority and financial assistance over a legal resident or a U.S. citizen.

While [President] Bush is having trouble mustering up Congressional support for amnesty, the process is underway nevertheless.

What you can't get by hook, you can get by crook.

If an illegal alien has a Mexican consular identification card, a driver's license and if his child qualifies for in-state tuition rates, he's got a good chunk of what amnesty would provide.

The Tuition Debate

Dozens of states are considering some or all of the above. In our own besieged California, consular identification cards are on the verge of statewide acceptance, driver's licenses for ille-

Joe Guzzardi, "View from Lodi, CA: Illegal Immigrants Will Take Americans' College Places—At Taxpayers' Expense," www.vdare.com, February 1, 2002. Reproduced by permission of the author.

gal aliens remain high on [former California] Governor Davis's wish list, and the Board of Regents approved in-state tuition at the prestigious University of California system last week in a 17-5 vote.

As with all immigration related issues in California, the dilemma of tuition breaks for bright, motivated but illegal students has plagued legislators for more than two decades.

In-state tuition for illegal immigrants is unfair across the board.

And, as usual in these debates, the ultimate outcome favored those here illegally.

Compassion has limits. California, already stretched to the maximum, should—but unceasingly refuses to—face reality.

An $11,000 discount in annual tuition to illegal aliens attending UC [University of California] schools does more than add to the state's looming $12 billion budget deficit. The message to illegal aliens sent by the Regents is clear: Come to California. College is on us!

In-state tuition for illegal immigrants is unfair across the board. Sometime soon, a legal California resident will lose his place at UC to an illegal alien. And that student's taxpaying parents will foot the bill.

Defending Tuition Breaks for Illegals

On January 22 [2002], CNN invited UC Regent Ward Connerly and [former Lieutenant] Governor Cruz Bustamante to debate tuition breaks for illegal immigrants. Anchor Jack Cafferty asked Bustamante . . . why taxpayers should have to subsidize college tuition for illegal aliens.

Said Bustamante elusively, "These young people are all in the process of being legalized."

"In that case," pressed Cafferty, "why not wait until they're legal?" Bustamante had no reply.

[In 2002], I spoke with two of the five Regents who voted against reduced tuition.

According to both, the Board of Regents caved in to heavy pressure from the Latino lobby. But neither "Nay" vote was cast because of strong-arming.

Both Regents felt that the decision to grant in-state tuition to illegal residents violated a federal law and would not hold up in court. A class action lawsuit filed by an out of state, legal U.S. resident who would not qualify for the same tuition break as an illegal alien is anticipated.

If you're wondering what could possibly be next in the continuing deference to illegal aliens, more bad news is right around the corner.

Generous Benefits for Illegals

Rep. Chris Cannon (R-UT), Bush's "point man" . . . , has introduced H. B. 1918, the Student Adjustment Act.

See if you can guess which way Cannon wants to adjust things.

H.B. 1918[1] would permit any high-school student illegally in the U.S. but with five years of good moral conduct to qualify for college financial aid including Pell Grants. Furthermore, those students would be exempt from deportation and could immediately apply for permanent residency.

Americans are overwhelmingly opposed to the entire bundle of bogus giveaways—consular visas, driver's licenses, in-state tuition and abundant welfare benefits now under consideration for legal immigrants but non-citizens. . . .

In a . . . public statement, Richard Riordan [an opponent of California governor Gray Davis in the 2002 gubernatorial recall election], expressed support for unlimited welfare and education benefits to illegal aliens.

Craven pandering has replaced common sense and fair play.

1. This act failed in 2001 but was reintroduced in 2003 as H.R. 1684. As of January 2006, the bill remains in committee.

7

The War on Terrorism Threatens the Rights of Illegal Immigrants

Nathan Newman

Nathan Newman, former vice president of the National Lawyers Guild, is a lawyer, writer, and community activist.

In the wake of the September 11, 2001, terrorist attacks, a growing anti-immigrant movement threatens illegal immigrant rights. Anti-immigrant policies do not, however, improve national security. In addition to increasing the dangers faced by illegal immigrants, they also drive them further underground, creating criminal networks where terrorists can operate. Policies that penalize employers who hire illegal workers do not guard against terrorism but leave illegal immigrants vulnerable to intimidation and exploitation in the workplace.

With exquisite opportunism, anti-immigrant groups have seized on the [terrorist] attacks of [September 11, 2001] to call for reversing the emerging movement for amnesty for the millions of undocumented immigrants in our country.

Anti-immigrant groups like the Federation for American Immigration Reform (FAIR) jumped to announce not only opposition to any plans for amnesty but support for new harsher laws to further harass millions of undocumented residents and to deny greater civil liberties to all Americans. Topping their list is a new national ID system that would allow

Nathan Newman, "A War on Immigrants to Fight the War on Terrorism," *Progressive Populist*, November 1, 2001. Reproduced by permission of the author.

the government to electronically track every citizen's and resident's movements, from where they are registered for school to where they work.

Given fears of terrorism, a lot of people may say a loss in civil liberties and privacy will be a small price to pay for greater security, but such a "solution" is a delusion, one that may lead to making the situation far worse. We've been down the road of promises that rolling back civil liberties was a short-cut to solving a broad-based problem—it's call the "war on drugs" and the results have been a minimal decrease in drug use but an explosion of organized crime and violence in the illegal underground bred by government policy.

One reason immigration amnesty had been gaining ground in policy circles is that, in areas ranging from public health to labor rights, many analysts had acknowledged that past policy had just encouraged an ever expanding ring of illegal exploiters, from smugglers to employers, feeding on the mass of vulnerable undocumented residents in legal limbo. Where the AFL-CIO [American Federation of Labor–Congress of Industrial Organizations] had once supported sanctions against employers of undocumented workers, new policy by the labor federation in support of amnesty was passed [in 2001] as union leaders saw that lesser rights for immigrants just turned them into easy targets for intimidation and sweatshop exploitation, often at the expense of other workers.

Cracking Down on Immigration

Cutting back immigrant rights is an even more dangerous policy in the context of threatened terrorism. A national ID or any other tool is unlikely to be a problem for terrorists backed by both cash and patience—no system is fool-proof and such a system is least likely to catch such targets. However, it will likely drive the millions of already existing undocumented immigrants further underground, creating a whole network of petty illegality where such terrorists would easily hide when needed with few questions asked.

A war on immigrants will be not only ineffective but fur-ther undermine our security by deepening the chasms of shadow existence in our midst.

That is the lesson of the drug war—the blurring of the lines between dangerous crime and petty actions just creates new arenas for illicit profit and expanding violence in society. You cannot criminalize the actions of millions of people with-out creating opportunities for extreme exploitation of those left with no recourse to normal channels of the law. Junkies turn to crime to pay for their habit, while undocumented im-migrants turn to smugglers and sweatshops to care for their families. Left with little alternative in a world of poverty and hunger in developing nations, such immigrants will come to the United States whatever the cost, but those costs will just end up mounting for the rest of society.

Unsurprisingly, terrorism has thrived on the underground institutions that have risen in the shadow of the drug war. Globally, the war on drugs has created massive profits to pay for the guns that fuel local violence. Little of the price paid on the streets of America goes to economic development in poor countries, but the "middle men" of smugglers skim their share, with some of those funds inevitably fueling violence of all kinds globally. Prohibition in the 1920s helped institutionalize organized crime in the United States while the drug war has done the same on a global scale. And terrorists have used that traffic to fund their efforts, unmoored from the need for sup-port from nation-states.

Adding to the Chaos

A new war on immigrants would merely add to the chaos and desperation on which terrorism feeds. There are tens of millions of refugees globally fleeing interstate violence and civil wars. Economic misery and desperation are driving tens of millions more out of their homes and countries. Even as we focus on the tragedy of September 11, we cannot ignore the millions of Afghanis displaced from decades of war in their homeland. In the face of such global misery, a war on immigrants will be not only ineffective but further undermine our security by deepening the chasms of shadow existence in our midst.

If the threat of physical terrorism will not be lessened by such attacks on immigrants and our own civil liberties, the threat of biological terrorism will be exponentially increased. With a strong public health system, the introduction of any biological agent poses relatively little threat, since any significantly lethal disease would be quickly detected and isolated. But as we isolate undocumented immigrants from that public health system (already often inadequate in our country), as a rigid national ID system would inevitably do, it increases the likelihood of disease, natural or terrorist-inspired, spreading without detection to the point it may be far harder to contain and far deadlier in its consequences.

Ultimately, the solution to drugs, excess immigration and terrorism share a basic approach—isolate the violent elements of any community while focusing on prevention and easing the misery that drives the problem and which the extreme elements exploit.

8

Strict Immigration Laws Are Necessary to Fight Terrorism

Mark Krikorian

Mark Krikorian is executive director of the Center for Immigration Studies, an organization that researches the effects of immigration on the United States and advocates for greater controls on immigration.

Most of the terrorists involved in the September 11, 2001, attacks on America had taken advantage of the nation's weak immigration enforcement system. Some had obtained temporary visas while others were applying for asylum or had entered the United States illegally. In order to prevent future attacks, immigration agencies should meticulously scrutinize the immigrants admitted to the country and rigorously monitor U.S. borders. Those fighting the war on terror at home need strict immigration policies to deny terrorists access to the United States.

> OH GOD, you who open all doors, please open all doors for me, open all venues for me, open all avenues for me.
>
> —Prayer found in [September 11, 2001, hijacker] Mohammed Atta's luggage.

Supporters of high immigration have tried to de-link immigration control from security. A week after the Sept. 11, 2001, hijackings, the head of the American Immigration Lawyers Association said, "I don't think [9/11] can be attributed to the failure of our immigration laws." Even the "9/11 Commission" —which in January [2004] held hearings on the im-

Mark Krikorian, "Safety Through Immigration Control," *The Providence Journal*, April 24, 2004. Reproduced by permission of the author.

migration failures that had contributed to the attacks—is devoting inordinate attention . . . to peripheral issues, such as who sent what memo to whom.

While ordinary people don't need hearings to know there's a link between immigration and security, a fuller understanding of the issue is necessary if we are to fix what needs to be fixed, and reduce the likelihood of future attacks.

Defending the Home Front

Deputy Defense Secretary Paul Wolfowitz said in October 2002:

"Sixty years ago, when we said, 'home front,' we were referring to citizens back home, doing their part to support the war front. Since last September, however, the home front has become a battlefront, every bit as real as any we've known before."

The reality of the home front isn't confined to the threat posed by Islamic terrorism. No enemy, whatever his ideology, has any hope of defeating America's armies in the field, and must therefore resort to what scholars call "asymmetric" or "fourth-generation" warfare: terrorism and related tactics, which we saw before 9/11 in the Mideast and East Africa, and which we are now seeing in Iraq. But the brass ring of such a strategy is mass killings of civilians on American soil.

Our enemies have repeatedly exercised [the] option of inserting terrorists by exploiting weaknesses in our immigration system.

Our objective on the home front is different from that faced by the military, because the goal is defensive: to block and disrupt the enemy's ability to carry out attacks on our territory. This will then allow offensive forces, if needed, to find, pin down and kill the enemy overseas.

Limiting Illegal Immigrant Rights Prevents Terrorism

So the burden of homeland defense is not borne by our armed forces but by agencies seen as civilian entities—mainly, the Department of Homeland Security. And of the DHS's many responsibilities, immigration control is central. The reason is elementary: No matter the weapon or delivery system—hijacked airliners, shipping containers, suitcase nukes, anthrax spores—terrorists are needed to carry out the attacks. And those terrorists have to enter and operate in the United States. In a very real sense, the primary weapons of our enemies are not the inanimate objects at all but, rather, the terrorists themselves, especially in the case of suicide attackers.

Thus, keeping the terrorists out, or apprehending them after they get in, is indispensable to victory. In the words of the administration's July 2002 "National Strategy for Homeland Security":

"Our great power leaves these enemies with few conventional options for doing us harm. One such option is to take advantage of our freedom and openness by secretly inserting terrorists into our country to attack our homeland. Homeland security seeks to deny this avenue of attack to our enemies and thus to provide a secure foundation for America's global engagement."

Our enemies have repeatedly exercised this option of inserting terrorists by exploiting weaknesses in our immigration system. A Center for Immigration Studies analysis found that nearly every element of the immigration system has been penetrated by the enemy. Of the 48 al-Qaida operatives who have committed terrorist acts here since 1993 (including the 9/11 hijackers), a third were here on various temporary visas, another third were legal residents or naturalized citizens, a fourth were illegal aliens, and the rest had pending asylum applications.

Nearly half of the total had, at some point or another, violated immigration laws.

A Comprehensive Approach

An immigration system designed for homeland security, therefore, needs to apply to all stages in the process: issuing visas overseas, screening people at the borders and airports, and enforcing the rules inside the country. Nor can we focus all our efforts on Mideasterners and ignore people from elsewhere; that may make sense in the short term—as triage, if you will—but in the longer term we need comprehensive improvements, because al-Qaida is adapting. The FBI has warned local law enforcement that al-Qaida is already exploring the use of Chechen terrorists, people with Russian passports who won't draw our attention if we're focusing mainly on Saudis and Egyptians.

None of this is to say that there are no other weapons against domestic terrorist attacks. We certainly need more effective international coordination, improved intelligence gathering and distribution, and special military operations. But in the end, the lack of effective immigration control leaves us naked in the face of the enemy.

9

Civilian Border Patrol Groups Threaten Illegal Immigrant Rights

Susy Buchanan and David Holthouse

Susy Buchanan and David Holthouse are senior writers for the Intelligence Report, *the quarterly magazine of the Southern Poverty Law Center's Intelligence Project, which monitors hate groups and extremist activity in the United States.*

The Minuteman Project, a civilian border patrol group that originated in Arizona in 2005, has sparked a series of spin-off groups in border and nonborder states alike. While these groups vary in the degree to which they advocate violence and spread racist rhetoric, they all threaten the rights of illegal immigrants. Some harass local establishments that serve illegal immigrants; others, inside observers allege, advocate killing immigrants attempting to cross the U.S.-Mexico border.

"Trigger happy," Gollad County, Texas, Sheriff Robert DeLaGarza thought to himself. It was early July [2005] and DeLaGarza was meeting with members of the Texas Minuteman Corps, a new vigilante border patrol outfit that started recruiting in DeLaGarza's county in June [2005].

"They kept talking a lot about shooting illegals, and what they could and couldn't do to make it self-defense of life or property," DeLaGarza said. "One woman kept asking, 'Well,

Susy Buchanan and David Holthouse, "Playing Rough," *Southern Poverty Law Center Intelligence Report*, fall 2005. Copyright © 2005 Southern Poverty Law Center. Reproduced by permission.

what if they reach for a rock, can we shoot them then? What if they're on private land? Can we shoot them for trespassing?'"

A chaotic army of [immigrant hunters] is on the march.

DeLaGarza gave the vigilantes a stern warning: "My community doesn't tolerate racism or racist violence in any form. I told them that if they step one inch out of line, I'm going to hammer their ass."

Violence on the Border

Later that month in California, two Mexicans were wounded in separate shootings the same night along a 14-mile stretch of the border between Campo and Tecate, Calif., that was being patrolled by the California Minutemen, another new vigilante border patrol group.

Both shootings occurred in the early hours of Saturday, July 23 [2005].

The first victim told investigators he was leading a group of illegal immigrants through the desert and was about 200 yards inside the United States when he heard a distant rifle shot and was struck in the buttocks by a single bullet. The second shooting took place one hour later. A group of eight adults and two children said they were huddled about 20 yards south of the border when a man wearing a mask and carrying a rifle suddenly appeared. When they ran, he fired a single shot, striking one of the men in the back of the leg.

Interviewed in the hospital by the *San Diego Union-Tribune*, the victim in the second shooting, 32-year-old Jose Humberto Rivera Perez of Guadalajara, disputed the claim by American and Mexican police that the gunman was most likely a bandit.

"If he were a bandit, he would have grabbed us and taken everything," Perez said. "He only shot at us and ran."

Humberto Garcia, the Tijuana-based regional coordinator for the Mexican government's National Human Rights Commission, said he feared the attack was either carried out or instigated by members of the California Minutemen, who he called *cazamigrantes* —"immigrant hunters."

"With this kind of operation, they are feeding feelings of hatred," Garcia said. "These feelings of hatred can inspire acts of violence like this. It's very strange that these acts are occurring in this context. We're not discarding any possibilities until the authorities find out who did this, one way or the other."

Minuteman groups in non-border states seem less focused on patrolling the border than generalized immigrant bashing.

The identity of the shooters may never be known. But this much is certain: a chaotic army of *cazamigrantes* is on the march.

The Immigrant Hunters

Inspired by the Minuteman Project, the month-long, much-hyped vigilante action held [in] Arizona in April [2005], more than 40 anti-immigration "citizens border patrol" and "internal vigilance" groups have formed since early May. The original Minuteman Project's leaders, Jim Gilchrist and Chris Simcox, have little or no control over most of these splinters, spin-offs and imitators.

Some are based in states with no Mexican borders to patrol. In Alabama, a group calling itself the Alabama Minutemen Support Team has pledged to recruit and train 125 "undocumented border patrol agents" for an October [2005] mission in New Mexico led by former antigovernment militia commander Mike Vanderboegh. Other Minuteman groups in non-border states seem less focused on patrolling the border than generalized immigrant bashing. In Tennessee, members of a group calling itself the Tennessee Volunteer Minutemen has been staking out day labor sites, harassing workers. The Utah Minutemen recently protested outside a bank in Salt Lake City that accepts Mexican consular identification cards for check-cashing purposes. And the Colorado Minutemen in July [2005] sponsored a demonstration outside the Denver Public Library to demand the removal of Mexican comic books from the shelves.

Minuteman groups have also formed in Maine, Michigan and Washington, and have announced plans to patrol the Canadian border this fall to protect America from invaders from the North. In Mobile, Ala., one Minuteman has taken it upon himself to ensure the Gulf waters are clear of invaders—by patrolling the seas armed with a Glock [pistol] and an M-16 [rifle].

But it is clearly along the southern border where Minutemen have the highest numbers of participants and the most militant supporters. Five of these spin-off groups are among the most important.

The California Minutemen Spark Controversy

Also dubbed California Border Watch and United States Border Patrol Auxiliary, the California Minutemen was founded by James Chase, a Vietnam veteran who says he was wounded six times in combat, then worked for the United States Postal Service until a nervous breakdown forced him to retire in 1997.

Chase was a prominent member of the original Minuteman Project in Arizona until he was injured in mid-April [2005] by a fall off a cliff. After recovering from his injuries, Chase launched California Minutemen with a Web site seeking "all those who do not want their family murdered by Al Qaeda, illegal migrants, colonizing illegal aliens, illegal alien felons, alien barbarians, Ninja-dressed drug smugglers" and "cowardly Aztlan punks and [revolutionary] Che Guevara pink pantied wimps lower than whale dung who should be fed to the chupacabra [a fictional, blood-sucking monster]!" Chase declared that unlike Gilchrist and Simcox, who at least articulated a handguns-only policy during their Arizona Minuteman Project (though it would be barely enforced), he would allow his recruits in California to openly carry hunting rifles, assault rifles and shotguns, though he also recommended bringing "baseball bats, stun guns, and machetes."

Gilchrist and Simcox quickly disowned Chase's group.

Citizen border patrol organizers . . . routinely refer to Mexican and Central America immigrants as 'invaders' and 'the enemy.'

"Mr. Chase has no authority to use the Minuteman Project name," Gilchrist declared in a June [2005] statement. "Neither does Mr. Chase have permission to trade upon the Arizona Minuteman Project's April record in any future border watch initiatives."

Says who? Gilchrist and Simcox had no legal grounds to dictate Chase's actions. They had no copyright on the concept of strapping on firearms and heading to the border for a migrant hunt. The movement they'd created had quickly slipped its leash, and Chase refused to obey their commands to heel.

"I keep hearing all these things: I'm a rogue. I'm a Rambo. I want to shoot the heads off people," Chase retorted in a June [2005] interview with the *San Diego Union-Tribune*. "I'm a [peace-loving] flower child compared to Gilchrist and Simcox." . . .

"If you are not a racist and have no desire to harm the harmless migrants, come and sign up," Chase posted to his Web site in August. "Remember: We are harmless as doves."

Friends of the Border Patrol Are Less Extreme

Founded by Andy Ramirez, a former minor league hockey goalie who ran unsuccessfully for the California state assembly twice in the 1990s, [the Friends of the Border Patrol] San Diego, Calif.–based group is supposed to begin operations along the Southern California border on Sept. 16, [2005] which is Mexico's Independence Day.

Ramirez's rhetoric is considerably more humanitarian than the language used by other citizen border patrol organizers, who routinely refer to Mexican and Central America immigrants as "invaders" and "the enemy." On his Web site, Ramirez states: "Mexico's elite must now reform their nation and share their wealth and reform their economy so their citizens can find hope and prosperity at home, without being enslaved and exploited after they illegally enter our country."

But despite his professed sympathy for his neighbors to the south, Ramirez has actively recruited Friends of the Border Patrol (FBP) volunteers from the ranks of the California Coalition for Immigration Reform, a hate group whose president, Barbara Coe, has repeatedly described Mexicans as "savages." . . .

Ramirez originally had planned to lead the California Minutemen along with Jim Chase. But in May [2005], Ramirez said he was disassociating himself from Chase because Chase condoned the use of violence and had suggested they secretly deploy snipers along the border. Chase has denied that accusation, saying it was a miscommunication. Ramirez insists he heard Chase correctly.

Eccentric Leads New Mexico Border Watch

Closely affiliated with Jim Chase's California Border Watch, this group formed in early June [2005] as New Mexico Minutemen, then changed its name when Simcox announced the

New Mexico Minuteman Corps as the "official" Minuteman patrol in New Mexico.

New Mexico Border Watch director "Chief Dr. Sir" Clifford Alford explains the rift between his group and Simcox, echoing the sentiments of others in the Minuteman movement who have been critical of Simcox and his arrogance. "Chris gets a bit high handed from time to time, as though groups should be 'sanctioned' by him," said Alford, who claims to be a Cherokee shaman, Wiccan sorcerer, Reiki [healing] master and newly ordained Templar knight [a Christian fraternal organization,] among other dubious titles. "Well, [Simcox] is not almighty God, and he is also not the Grand Prior of the Knights Templar, so pardon me if I don't give a flip."

A self-proclaimed (and highly paranoid) expert on the occult, Alford has conducted law enforcement training seminars on Satanism and "Ninja death cults" he said were being secretly trained to spearhead a mass slaughter across the globe. . . .

The Texas Minuteman Corps Appears Racist

In early June [2005], Chris Simcox appointed Goliad County, Texas, petroleum engineer Bill Parmley to be president of the Texas Minuteman Corps. Two months later, Parmley resigned, citing widespread racism among the group's volunteers, who Parmley said were more anti-Hispanic than anti–illegal immigration. Parmley alleged that many of the volunteers hatched a plot to force all the Hispanic elected officials in Goliad County from office and replace them exclusively with Caucasians.

The first to use Minutemen [border patrol] tactics were Klansmen.

"I don't know of any other word to describe it than racism," Parmley later told the *Fort Worth Weekly*. "They had a secret agenda before the organization ever got started. They rolled it into the Minutemen."

One of the Hispanic officials the Minutemen were out to get, Goliad County Sheriff DeLaGarza, said that after he met with the citizen border patrol members and fielded their eager questions about the legal use of deadly force, he did his best to dampen their trigger happiness with his threat to "hammer their ass."

The left-wing Brown Berets also recently sent the Texas Minuteman Corps a warning of their own. "Think twice before you come here," Brown Berets leader Pablo Delgado said at a July 28 [2005] news conference. Delgado said members of the militant Chicano organization are forming their own civilian border patrols, and will be active on the Texas border in October [2005] when Texas Minuteman Corps is scheduled to being operations at the same time as Simcox-sanctioned outfits in Arizona and New Mexico.

"We will be armed," Delgado said, "and we will use whatever force is necessary to defend the lives of immigrants."

Running Against Immigrants

The first to use Minutemen tactics were Klansmen.

In 1977, Ku Klux Klan leaders David Duke and Tom Metzger formed Klan Border Watch, a KKK vigilante border patrol in southern California. Like [the April 2005] Minuteman Project in Arizona, Klan Border Watch was primarily a media stunt designed to fan the flames of anti-immigration sentiment in America and to generate publicity for its ambitious leaders. Three years later, Metzger ran for Congress in California on the promise that he would militarize the border. Running openly as a Klansman, Metzger, who was then Duke's California state leader, would garner 33,000 votes, although he lost the election.

Taking a page from Metzger's playbook, three Minuteman group founders ran for state office, and Jim Gilchrist declared himself a Constitution Party candidate for the special congressional election in his Orange County, Calif., district to fill the seat vacated when President Bush appointed former Congressman Chris Cox to head the Securities and Exchange Commission.

Simcox, meanwhile, hired a public relations specialist and hinted at a congressional campaign of his own. Lauded as a hero at anti-immigration rallies across the country, Simcox also benefited from glowing coverage provided to millions of Fox News Channel viewers in a three-night special report from the border hosted by conservative pundit Sean Hannity that screened like a recruitment infomercial for the Minuteman movement.

Despite being decried by President Bush, border vigilantism has already been endorsed by sitting Republican congressmen, including Tom Tancredo of Colorado, who is almost certain to run for president on an anti-immigration platform, and by John Culberson of Texas, who on July 28 [2005] introduced legislation that would allocate $6.8 million in federal funds to establish armed citizen militias in borders states. The militias' members would be empowered to arrest illegal immigrants using "any means and force authorized by state law."

Forty-seven lawmakers have already agreed to co-sponsor the "Border Protection Corps Act."

But the leaders of the Minuteman movement aren't waiting for federal authorization. In late June [2005], addressing a crowd of 300 new Minuteman recruits in Goliad, Texas, Simcox delivered this ultimatum: "If we don't see the National Guard and the U.S. military on the border by October, we're going to patrol the border with 20,000 citizens. That will be a warning. In six months, if we don't see the military on the border, you might be faced with an army of 100,000 citizens."

10

Civilian Border Patrol Groups Protect U.S. Borders

Hillary Pate

Hillary Pate is an intern at the Heritage Foundation, a conservative public policy think tank in Washington, D.C.

Civilian border patrol groups are necessary to monitor illegal immigration across the U.S.-Mexico border since the U.S. government has thus far failed to do so. These groups protect the border from immigrants who would exploit opportunities and benefits paid for by American taxpayers. Critics claim that civilian border patrol groups act as vigilantes. However, these groups do not take the law into their own hands; they are simply assisting the U.S. Border Patrol by reporting illegal immigrant sightings. In fact, no evidence exists of civilian border groups using their firearms to injure illegal immigrants.

Those who can, do. And those who can't, criticize.

Maybe that explains why some citizens—even President Bush—are carping at the "Minuteman Project," which has attracted volunteers nationwide in an effort to prevent illegal immigrants from entering the United States.

An April 11 [2005], editorial in *The New York Times* is a good example. The *Times* describes the Minutemen as "a few dozen gunslingers patrolling for illegal immigrants," and claims these civilians "would be far saner to leave the patrolling of the border to the border patrol."

Hillary Pate, "Minutemen, or Men of the Minute?," www.heritage.org, April 26, 2005. Copyright © 2005, The Heritage Foundation. All rights reserved. Reproduced by permission.

Of course, that's something the Minutemen would be happy to do—if the border patrol was actually doing the job.

It may be difficult for a person sitting behind a desk in a Manhattan skyscraper to realize, but illegal immigration is a huge and growing problem in many states. Some of us in Arizona have actually watched illegal immigrants cross the border, and we're tired of it.

Enforcers, Not Vigilantes

The Minutemen aren't "vigilantes" out to kill people who cross the borders. They simply want to see that the law is upheld. It's not something they would have to worry about if the president and Congress had not neglected to enforce it—the unfortunate case so far.

There have been no incidents where Minuteman volunteers have used their firearms to harm illegal immigrants.

"We're not gunslingers," says Gray Deacon, a retiree and Minuteman volunteer. According to Deacon, while a few of the volunteers do carry arms, it's for protection against dangerous animals, including snakes, mountain lions and coyotes, all of which are common along the border.

Americans shouldn't think of these volunteers as "vigilantes." They're citizens trying desperately to protect the west from a human tide of illegals. And they're not getting as much help as they need.

The Minutemen say members of the ACLU [American Civil Liberties Union] in Arizona have actually helped some 100 illegal immigrants escape after these fugitives were reported to authorities.

On the other hand, the Minutemen merely report any illegal immigrants they spot to the border patrol. And Gray Deacon maintains that the volunteers have no physical contact with the illegals. "We are here to watch, spot, report and assist the border patrol," he says. Minutemen volunteers have even provided water, food and medical treatment to the illegal immigrants while they were waiting for the border patrol to arrive.

Furthermore, Andy Adame, spokesperson for the Tucson sector of the border patrol, says there have been no incidents where Minuteman volunteers have used their firearms to harm illegal immigrants. None.

Separating Legal and Illegal Immigration

Now, some people might think that these Minutemen and others who are trying to stop illegal immigration are racist or anti-immigration. So it's worth remembering that there's a difference between illegal and legal immigration—although the line has been blurred somewhat by our inability to enforce the law over the years.

This isn't to say there shouldn't be any immigration. After all, our country was founded on the concept of migration and immigration. But since the founding of our nation, immigration has been restricted by laws. Too many today are crossing illegally.

The Minuteman volunteers are working alongside the border patrol in an attempt to enforce the existing immigration law, and to make a point to Congress while doing so. So far, those efforts seem to be paying off. According to the Minuteman Project's Web site, border apprehensions have dropped from approximately 256 per day in April 2004 to 158 per day so far in April 2005.

Fewer people are trying to cross because more eyes are looking for illegals. Minutemen reported 241 illegal immigrants since they started the project on April 5, including one "coyote," the term applied to people who make their living transporting illegal immigrants to different destinations throughout the West.

Anyone who doubts the importance of the Minutemen's efforts ought to spend one day in Nogales, Tombstone, Sierra Vista or Douglas, Ariz. Most people, I think, would find it surprising to see how routinely border security is flouted.

And not just by people who pose a physical threat. While visiting a nearby school district last year, for example, I saw an SUV stop on the border, just a few miles from a border-patrol checkpoint. A small girl, pink backpack in hand, got out and raced to a nearby school bus.

A principal at the girl's elementary school says she doesn't mind the fact that there are illegal children attending the school. In fact, she welcomes them. This principal had even personally driven a student to the border after school one day.

Something's wrong with this picture, especially since American taxpayers are footing the bill for these children's education.

Too many illegals cross the border daily. The Minutemen want to change that. Far from being vigilantes, these people are law-abiding citizens, who aim to see our laws enforced. Hopefully, lawmakers in Washington will rise to their defense.

11

Illegal Immigrants Should Be Issued Driver's Licenses

American Immigration Lawyers Association

The American Immigration Lawyers Association is a national association of attorneys and law professors who practice and teach immigration law and whose goal is to convince the American people and elected leaders that immigration brings many benefits to U.S. society.

Proposals to restrict the right of illegal immigrants to obtain driver's licenses will not increase national security. In fact, such proposals will impede law enforcement and make Americans less safe. Denying illegal immigrants driver's licenses increases the number of fraudulent identity documents, which frustrates efforts to track foreign nationals within U.S. borders. Issuing driver's licenses to illegal immigrants, on the other hand, allows law enforcement to verify the identity of those within the nation's borders. Moreover, refusing to issue driver's licenses to illegal immigrants increases the number of unlicensed drivers, making U.S. roads less safe for American drivers.

The U.S. Congress and state legislatures have begun considering measures to restrict immigrants' access to driver's licenses.[1] These proposals go well beyond denying undocumented immigrants access to driver's licenses and are likely to affect legal immigrants and even U.S. citizens. While intended

1. For the most recent status of state driver's license legislation see the National Immigration Law Center Web site link: www.nilc.org/immspbs/DLs/index.htm#statereqs.

"Economic Outlook Shows Vital Need for Immigrants in U.S. Economy," American Immigration Lawyers Association, 2004. Copyright © 2004, American Immigration Lawyers Association. Reproduced by permission.

to increase national security, these measures will not enhance our security but will interfere with effective law enforcement.

Ineffective and Invasive Proposals

The September 11 [2001] terrorist attacks have led to renewed calls for a national identification (ID) system. However, since national ID proposals have been defeated in the past, proponents are seeking to develop such a national system indirectly, through existing forms of ID such as state driver's licenses. The American Association of Motor Vehicle Administrators (AAMVA) is urging the federal government to fund and authorize a proposal to standardize state driver's licenses. The AAMVA . . . announced that it supports uniform standards for driver's licenses across all fifty states. If implemented, uniform driver's licenses would result in a de facto national ID card.

Denying driver's licenses to large segments of the population is an inefficient way to enforce immigration laws and prevent terrorism.

Representative Jeff Flake (R-AZ) introduced H.R. 4043 in March of 2002. This measure would bar federal agencies from accepting for any identification-related purpose any state-issued driver's license, or other comparable identification document, unless the state requires that such licenses or documents issued to nonimmigrant aliens expire upon the expiration of the aliens' nonimmigrant visas. [As of January 2006, this bill remains in the House Judiciary Committee.]

At the same time, some state officials have linked the denial of driver's licenses to undocumented immigrants to efforts to combat terrorism, alleging that the driver's licenses that several of the terrorists obtained facilitated their activities. (However, the terrorists did not need U.S. issued driver's licenses to board planes on September 11 because they had foreign passports that would have enabled them to board.)

Since September 11, many states are considering proposals to tighten the rules regarding driver's license eligibility and to further restrict immigrants' access to driver's licenses.

AILA [American Immigration Lawyers Association] opposes limiting immigrants' access to driver's licenses based on immigration status. Denying driver's licenses to large segments of the population is an inefficient way to enforce immigration and prevent terrorism and would make everyone in the community less safe.

Impeding Law Enforcement

Restrictive Licensing Will Impede Law Enforcement and National Security. Many local law enforcement officials oppose restrictive licensing proposals because driver's license databases play an important role in enforcement. Restrictive proposals will undermine law enforcement because:

- Licensing noncitizens enriches our domestic intelligence by allowing law enforcement authorities to verify and obtain the identities, residences, and addresses of millions of foreign nationals. Restrictive licensing will deprive authorities of this information.

- The proliferation of fraudulent documents that will result from restrictive licensing will impede law enforcement efforts by contaminating intelligence regarding who is present in the United States.

Proposals to restrict immigrants' access to driver's licenses will result in more unlicensed drivers operating vehicles on U.S. roads.

State Driver's License Agencies Have Neither the Authorization nor Knowledge to Interpret Immigration Laws and Documents. Restrictive licensing will require state motor vehicle administrators to become INS [Immigration and Naturalization Service] law and document experts in order to evaluate properly an applicant's immigration status and determine when such status expires. Immigration law creates approximately 60 ever-changing nonimmigrant visa categories in addition to classifications for asylees, refugees, parolees, persons in immigration proceedings, persons under orders of supervision, and applicants for many of these categories, as well as applicants for extension, change, or adjustment of status, to name a few. The scheme of documents issued by the INS, the State Department, and other agencies as evidence of these classifications is even more perplexing and includes visa stamps, laminated cards, unlaminated handwritten cards, forms, letters, and many other documents, either in combination or alone, which, even to the trained eye, often do not clearly show an applicant's status or duration of admission. Additionally, due to extensive INS delays in application processing, many immigrants and lawful nonimmigrants will be unable to present documentation of their status. It is highly unlikely that motor vehicle administrators will be able to determine correctly whether a particular document or combination of documents establishes lawful status. This task requires the interpretation and application of a complex body of law. Requiring DMV [department of motor vehicles] personnel to understand and enforce immigration laws will most likely result in legal United States residents facing wrongful license denials and revocations for reasons that are wholly unrelated to driver competence.

Jeopardizing Safety and Security

Restrictive Licensing Will Severely Jeopardize Highway Safety. Proposals to restrict immigrants' access to driver's licenses will result in more unlicensed drivers operating vehicles on U.S. roads. Whether licensed or not, many individuals will have no choice but to drive—to work, to schools, to doctors, and to many other destinations—to meet basic everyday needs. Thus, restrictive licensing has the potential to reduce the safety of Americans and all drivers on our roads because it will:

- Remove an entire segment of the driving population from the reach of administrators charged with testing and certifying driver competence, which will contribute to the national highway mortality rate of 40,000 persons each year;

- Deprive motor vehicle administrators of the driving records of millions of drivers;

- Discourage or prevent millions of drivers from registering their vehicles;

- Eliminate incentives for foreign nationals to attend driver education schools;

- Increase the rate of minor traffic violations for unlicensed driving, which will divert law enforcement and judicial resources from truly serious offenses; and

- Create incentives for unlicensed drivers to flee accident scenes.

Denying driver's licenses based on immigration status also will prevent millions of drivers from obtaining insurance, which will increase uninsured motorist pools, contribute to current uninsured motorist losses of $4.1 billion, and increase insurance rates.

Production and Sale of Falsified Documents Is Likely to Increase If Larger Numbers of Noncitizens Are Denied Driver's Licenses. Restrictive licensing will encourage the fraudulent production and use of the many documents that are available to establish lawful immigration status by transforming the driver's license into a de facto INS document that will become necessary to establish lawful status. These fraudulent documents will further complicate the task of motor vehicle administrators by requiring them to detect fraudulent INS documents. Additionally, restrictive licensing will increase the market for easily obtained fraudulent documents, such as birth certificates and social security numbers, to establish identity. According to the Department of Health and Human Services, there are 14,000 different versions of birth certificates currently in circulation.

12

Illegal Immigrants Should Not Be Issued Driver's Licenses

D.A. King

D.A. King is founder of the American Resistance, an organization that works to combat illegal immigration. He writes for Michnews.com and vdare.com, an anti–illegal immigration Web site.

Driver's licenses are a widely accepted form of identification in the United States and are easy for illegal immigrants to obtain. In fact, the September 11, 2001 terrorist attacks were facilitated by the terrorists' ability to obtain driver's licenses upon their illegal entry into the United States. The Intel Bill, a proposal that would deny driver's licenses to illegal immigrants, would have improved U.S. security. Unfortunately, the bill failed in 2004.

Question: What was one of the first things that the 9/11 murderers did when they were allowed to enter our nation?

Answer: Obtain a driver's license—the universally accepted identifier in our country.

Between them, the 19 America-hating highjackers had no difficulty in collecting sixty-three driver's licenses from several states, including Florida, New Jersey and Virginia. At present, 11 states issue driver's licenses to illegal aliens.

D. A. King, "Feds Are the Problem, Not the Cure, on Illegal Immigration," *Marietta Daily Journal*, Marietta, GA, December 8, 2004. Reproduced by permission of the author.

Limiting Licenses Fights Illegal Immigration

That is important to note in light of the recent Congressional fight over the Intelligence Reform and Terrorism Prevention Act of 2004 (the "Intel Bill")—a piece of legislation that came out of the U.S. House as HR 10, which had taken recommendations from the summer's 9/11 Commission study.

One of those recommendations was that the federal government standardize the requirements for each of our 50 states for the issuance of a driver's license.

There was a provision in the bill that would have banned the issuance of a driver's license to people who reside in America illegally. It was a provision that would have made our national standards for a driver's license nearly as secure as those of Mexico's and greatly increased our internal security.

The president of the United States [George W. Bush] led the fight to remove the provision that would deny driver's licenses to illegal aliens in the United States.

It was a provision that would have made life much more complicated for what Georgia state Sen. Sam Zamarippa estimates to be the more than 20 million illegal aliens in our nation.

Limiting Illegal Immigration Fights Terrorism

However, it was a provision that would have made it more difficult for the president to operate the ongoing illegal labor auction that benefits the corporations that contribute millions of dollars to both political parties.

The horror of the events of 9/11 should have changed our national security and border enforcement practices forever. It did not. Since then, illegal immigration has *increased* and in the year 2003, two states, New Mexico and Maryland, actually passed laws allowing illegals to obtain a driver's license.

Against strong and constant opposition, the Chairman of the House Judiciary Committee, Congressman James Sensenbrenner (R- Wis.), led a heroic but futile fight to keep the provision in the bill that was aimed at overhauling our internal security.

From where did the opposition come? Who would publicly oppose an effort to deny illegal aliens the document that we use to board a plane, purchase explosives and weapons, wire money and generally blend into mainstream America?

Here is a quote from U.S. Senator Susan Collins (R-Maine) regarding the driver's license provision that she helped kill— "These were highly controversial and divisive provisions, many of which were opposed by the administration."

The president of the United States led the fight to remove the provision that would deny driver's licenses to illegal aliens in the United States.

An action alert from The National Council of The Race (aka "La Raza"), an organization devoted to assisting illegal aliens and one that works tirelessly to obtain for them the rights of citizens, calls the provision "ill-conceived, anti-immigrant and anti-civil liberty."

Securing U.S. Borders

U.S. Rep. Tom Tancredo (R-Colorado), a leader in the fight to secure American borders and enforce our immigration laws, is quoted as saying, "Securing the borders is a philosophical problem for the president. He is an 'open borders' guy, and that's just it."

It is difficult to guess in which camp [Republican or Democrat] the largest sigh of relief was heard when the final vote was made in the U.S. Senate: the boardrooms of corporate America, the offices of the vast illegal alien lobby, or the White House.

As someone who has regular contact with Georgia state legislators, I hope that I can remain polite and respectful the next time one of them attempts to dodge the hard decisions that must be made on a state level regarding the illegal immigration crisis in Georgia by dismissing it with the remark that "illegal immigration is a federal problem."

As was demonstrated on the Intel Bill, the federal government *is* the problem.

For this angry American, securing our republic is not "controversial" or "divisive."

What would our grandfathers say? What will our children say?

Organizations to Contact

American Civil Liberties Union (ACLU)
125 Broad St., 18th Floor, New York, NY 10004
(212) 549-2585
Web site: www.aclu.org

The ACLU is a national organization that champions the rights found in the Declaration of Independence and the U.S. Constitution. The ACLU Immigrants' Rights Project works with refugees and immigrants facing deportation and with immigrants in the workplace. It has published reports, position papers, and books, some of which are available on its Web site, detailing what freedoms immigrants and refugees have under the U.S. Constitution.

American Immigration Lawyers Association (AILA)
918 F St. NW, Washington, DC 20004
(202) 216-2400 • fax: (202) 783-7853
Web site: www.aila.org

AILA is a professional association of lawyers who work in the field of immigration and nationality law. It publishes the *AILA Immigration Journal* and compiles and distributes a continuously updated bibliography of government and private documents on immigration laws and regulations.

The American Resistance Foundation
3595 Canton Rd., A-9 / PMB337, Marietta, GA 30066
fax: (770) 427-9998
Web site: www.theamericanresistance.com

The mission of the American Resistance Foundation is to fight what it believes is an immigrant invasion by securing U.S. borders, enforcing U.S. laws, and denying amnesty to illegal immigrants. The foundation's Web site contains a collection of articles that elaborate its mission.

Americans for Immigration Control (AIC)
PO Box 738, Monterey, VA   24465
(540) 468-2023 • fax: (540) 468-2026
e-mail: aic@immigrationcontrol.com
Web site: www.immigrationcontrol.com

AIC lobbies Congress to adopt legal reforms that would reduce U.S. immigration. It calls for increased funding for the
U.S. Border Patrol and the deployment of military forces to
prevent illegal immigration. It also supports sanctions against
employers who hire illegal immigrants and opposes amnesty
for such immigrants. On its Web site AIC publishes articles
such as "Erasing America: The Politics of the Borderless Nation."

The Brookings Institution
1775 Massachusetts Ave. NW, Washington, DC   20036
(202) 797-6000 • fax: (202) 797-6004
e-mail: brookinfo@brookings.edu
Web site: www.brook.edu

The Brookings Institution, founded in 1927, is a liberal research and education organization that publishes material on
economics, government, and foreign policy. It publishes analy-
ses of immigration issues in its quarterly journal, *Brookings
Review*, and in various articles, books, commentary, reports,
and speeches, including titles such as "Combating the Illegal
Employment of Foreign Workers."

Cato Institute
1000 Massachusetts Ave. NW, Washington, DC   20001-5403
(202) 842-0200 • fax: (202) 842-3490
Web site: www.cato.org

The Cato Institute is a libertarian public policy research foundation dedicated to stimulating policy debate. It believes immigration is good for the U.S. economy and favors easing immigration restrictions. In addition to various articles on

immigration, the institute publishes Julian L. Simon's book *The Economic Consequences of Immigration*. On its Web site the institute publishes studies and commentary on immigration issues.

Center for Immigration Studies

1522 K St. NW, Suite 820, Washington, DC   20005-1202
(202) 466-8185 • fax: (202) 466-8076
e-mail: center@cis.org
Web site: www.cis.org

The Center for Immigration Studies examines the effects of immigration on the economic, social, demographic, and environmental conditions in the United States. Believing that the large number of recent immigrants has become a burden on America, the center favors reforming immigration laws to make them more consistent with U.S. interests. The center publishes editorials, reports, and position papers.

Federation for American Immigration Reform (FAIR)

1666 Connecticut Ave. NW, Suite 400
   Washington, DC   20009
(202) 328-7004 • fax: (202) 387-3447
e-mail: info@fairus.org
Web site: www.fairus.org

FAIR works to stop illegal immigration and limit legal immigration. It believes that the growing flood of immigrants into the United States causes higher unemployment and taxes social services. FAIR publishes a monthly newsletter, reports, and position papers, including *Running in Place: Immigration and U.S. Energy Usage* and *Invitation to Terror: How Our Immigration System Still Leaves America at Risk*, which are available on its Web site.

The Heritage Foundation
214 Massachusetts Ave. NE, Washington, DC   20002-4999
(202) 546-4400 • fax: (202) 546-8328
e-mail: info@heritage.org
Web site: www.heritage.org

The Heritage Foundation is a conservative public policy research institute. It has published articles on immigration in its
Backgrounder series and in its quarterly journal, *Policy Review*. Articles and reports on immigration can be found using
the searchable database on its Web site.

The Migration Policy Institute
1400 Sixteenth St. NW, Suite 300, Washington, DC   20036
(202) 266-1940 • fax: (202) 266-1900
e-mail: info@migrationpolicy.org
Web site: www.migrationpolicy.org

The Migration Policy Institute is an independent think tank
that examines the movement of people throughout the world.
It studies immigration policy issues, including how to manage
North American borders and how to strike a balance between
national security and civil liberties. The institute has published a series of migration studies indicating that border enforcement alone is not sufficient to curtail illegal migration.

The Minuteman Civil Defense Corps
6501 Greenway Pkwy., Suite 103-640, Scottsdale, AZ   85254
(520) 457-2320
e-mail: info@MinutemanHQ.com
Web site: www.minutemanhq.com

The Minuteman Civil Defense Corps is a group of civilian
volunteers working to implement the Minuteman Project, a
plan to stem the flow of illegal immigrants across U.S. borders. The corps' goal is to amplify the work of the U.S. Border
Patrol in protecting U.S. citizens from illegal immigrants who
"take advantage of a free American society." Its Web site publishes articles highlighting Minuteman activities nationwide.

National Council of La Raza (NCLR)

1126 Sixteenth St. NW, Washington, DC   20036
(202) 785-1670
Web site: www.nclr.org

NCLR seeks to improve opportunities for Americans of Hispanic descent. It conducts research on immigration and opposes restrictive immigration laws. The council publishes and distributes congressional testimony and policy reports, including *A License to Break the Law? Protecting the Integrity of Driver's Licenses and Immigration Enforcement by Local Police: The Impact on the Civil Rights of Latinos.*

National Immigration Forum

50 F St., Suite 300, Washington, DC   20001
(202) 347-0047 • fax: (202) 347-0058
e-mail: info@immigrationforum.org
Web site: www.immigrationforum.org

The National Immigration Forum believes that immigration strengthens America and that welfare benefits do not attract illegal immigrants. It supports effective measures aimed at curbing illegal immigration and promotes programs and policies that help refugees and immigrants assimilate into American society. The forum publishes the annual *Immigration Policy Handbook* as well as editorials, press releases, and fact sheets, many of which are available using the Web site's searchable database.

National Network for Immigrant and Refugee Rights (NNIRR)

310 Eighth St., Suite 303, Oakland, CA   94607
(510) 465-1984 • fax: (510) 465-1885
e-mail: nnirr@nnirr.org
Web site: www.nnirr.org

NNIRR includes community, church, labor, and legal groups committed to the cause of equal rights for all immigrants. These groups work to end discrimination and unfair treatment of illegal immigrants and refugees by strengthening and coordinating educational efforts among immigration advocates nationwide. NNIRR's legalization project aims to provide legal residency status to undocumented immigrants. Recent issues of the network's monthly newsletter, *Network News*, are available on its Web site.

Negative Population Growth Inc. (NPG)
2861 Duke St., Suite 36, Alexandria, VA   22314
(703) 370-9510 • fax: (703) 370-9514
e-mail: npg@npg.org
Web site: www.npg.org

NPG believes that world population must be reduced and calls for limiting legal immigration and thwarting illegal immigration. The methods it advocates to stop illegal immigration include increased border enforcement, improved identification of illegal aliens, and better detection of visa abusers. NPG publishes position papers on population and immigration in its *NPG Forum*. It also publishes a quarterly newsletter, *Population and Resource Outlook*, recent issues of which are available on its Web site.

Numbers USA
1601 N. Kent St., Suite 1100, Arlington, VA   22209
(703) 816-8820
e-mail: info@numbersusa.com
Web site: www.NumbersUSA.com

Numbers USA opposes the use of federal immigration policies to fuel U.S. population growth and to decrease wages. It tracks the number of legal and illegal immigrants entering the United States and seeks to educate the public about ways to lower immigration numbers, both legal and illegal, without advocating hostility toward immigrants. Reports such as *Illegal Immigration Is Not a Victimless Crime* are available on its Web site.

Public Policy Institute of California (PPIC)
500 Washington St., Suite 800, San Francisco, CA 94111
(415) 291-4400 • fax: (415) 291-4401
Web site: www.ppic.org

PPIC works to improve California's public policy through nonpartisan research on important issues. Its immigration research focuses on the 30 percent of Californian immigrants it estimates to be undocumented and the impact on border enforcement policy, education policy, and California's communities. PPIC immigration reports include titles such as *Holding the Line? The Effect of Recent Border Build-Up on Unauthorized Immigration and Undocumented Immigration to California: 1980–1993*.

U. S. Citizenship and Immigration Service (USCIS)
U.S. Department of Homeland Security
  Washington, DC 20528
Web site: www.uscis.gov

The USCIS, part of the Department of Homeland Security, is charged with administrative and management functions and responsibilities that were once handled by the former Immigration and Naturalization Service, including enforcement of immigration laws and regulations and the administration of immigrant-related services such as the granting of asylum and refugee status. USCIS produces numerous reports and evaluations on selected programs. Statistics and information on immigration and immigration laws are available on its Web site.

U.S. Immigration and Customs Enforcement (ICE)
425 I St. NW, Washington, DC 20536
Web site: www.ice.gov

A division of Border and Transportation Security (BTS) under the Department of Homeland Security, ICE has the specific mission of preventing terrorism by tracking people, money, and materials involved in terrorist acts. One of its responsibilities is to remove unauthorized aliens from the United

States. The "ICE Storm" initiative aims to thwart criminal smuggling of illegal aliens in the Phoenix, Arizona, area. The ICE Web site contains many press releases and articles related to border security, as well as the newsletter *Inside ICE*.

Bibliography

Books

Roy Beck   *The Case Against Immigration.* New York: W.W. Norton, 1996.

Nicholas Capaldi   *Immigration: Debating the Issues.* Amherst, NY: Prometheus, 1997.

Steve Cohen   *No One Is Illegal: Asylum and Immigration Control Past and Present.* Stoke on Trent, UK: Trentham, 2003.

Wayne A. Cornelius et al., eds.   *Controlling Immigration: A Global Perspective.* Palo Alto, CA: Stanford University Press, 2004.

Debra L. DeLaet   *U.S. Immigration Policy in an Age of Rights.* Westport, CT: Praeger, 2000.

John E. Dougherty   *Illegals: The Imminent Threat Posed by Our Unsecured U.S.-Mexico Border.* Nashville: WND, 2004.

Mark Dow   *American Gulag: Inside US Immigration Prisons.* Berkeley: University of California Press, 2004.

William Dudley, ed.   *Illegal Immigration.* San Diego: Greenhaven, 2002.

Samuel T. Francis   *America Extinguished: Mass Immigration and the Disintegration of American Culture.* Monterey VA: AIC Foundation, 2002.

Louise I. Gerdes, ed.	*Immigration*. San Diego: Greenhaven, 2005.
Jennifer Gordon	*Suburban Sweatshops: The Fight for Immigrant Rights*. Cambridge, MA: Harvard University Press, 2005.
Michelle Malkin	*Invasion: How America Still Welcomes Terrorists, Criminals, and Other Foreign Menaces to Our Shores*. Washington, DC: Regnery, 2002.
Joel Millman	*The Other Americans*. New York: Penguin, 1997.
Claudia Schlosberg	*Immigrant Access to Health Benefits: A Resource Manual*. Washington, DC: National Health Law Program, 2002.
Peter H. Schuck	*Citizens, Strangers, and In-Betweens: Essays on Immigration and Citizenship*. Boulder, CO: Westview, 2000.

Periodicals

Dick Ahles	"UConn to Assess a Policy on Illegal Immigrants," *New York Times*, March 7, 2004.
Lizette Alvarez and John M. Broder	"More and More, Women Risk All to Enter U.S.," *New York Times*, January 10, 2006.
Nina Bernstein	"Immigrants Face Loss of Licenses in ID Crackdown," *New York Times*, August 19, 2004.

Jim F. Couch, J. Douglas Barrett, and Peter M. Williams	"Total Amnesty for Illegal Aliens?" *World & I*, February 2004.
Robert Davis	"Health Care, Without Question," *USA Today*, September 6, 2001.
Michael Arnold Glueck	"High Cost of Medical Care for Illegal Immigrants," Newsmax.com, December 27, 2005.
Steven Greenhouse	"Immigrant Workers Share a Bus and Hopes," *New York Times*, September 28, 2003.
Steven Greenhouse	"Rewards of a 90-Hour Week: Poverty and Dirty Laundry," *New York Times*, May 31, 2004.
Victor Davis Hanson	"California, Here They Come (and Come): E Pluribus Unum Is Losing to La Raza," *National Review*, August 11, 2003.
Simon Houpt	"Workers' Rights: On the Table," *Globe & Mail*, February 28, 2005.
Gerald F. Kicanas	"Never Again! Illegal Immigrants in the U.S. Face Conditions Similar to Those in Concentration Camps," *America*, November 3, 2003.
Christopher Marquis	"At Border, Fortification Conflicts with Compassion," *New York Times*, May 25, 2001.

Laura Parker	"USA Just Wouldn't Work Without Immigrant Labor," *USA Today*, July 22, 2001.
Margot Roosevelt	"Border War in Arizona," *Time*, October 11, 2004.
Margot Roosevelt	"Illegal but Fighting for Rights," *Time*, January 22, 2001.
Charlie Savage	"Congress Set to Impose ID Card Rules," *Boston Globe*, May 5, 2005.
Jerry Seper	"Border Patrol Told to Stand Down in Arizona," *Washington Times*, May 13, 2005.
Mary Beth Sheridan and Nurith C. Aizenman	"Bush Immigration Plan Greeted with Joy, Skepticism," *Washington Post*, January 8, 2004.
Rebecca Smith	"Immigrants' Right to Workers' Comp," *Trial*, April 1, 2004.
Rachel L. Swarns	"Bill on Illegal-Immigrant Aid Draws Fire," *New York Times*, December 30, 2005.
Rachel L. Swarns	"Tough Border Security Bill Nears Passage in the House," *New York Times*, December 14, 2005.

Index